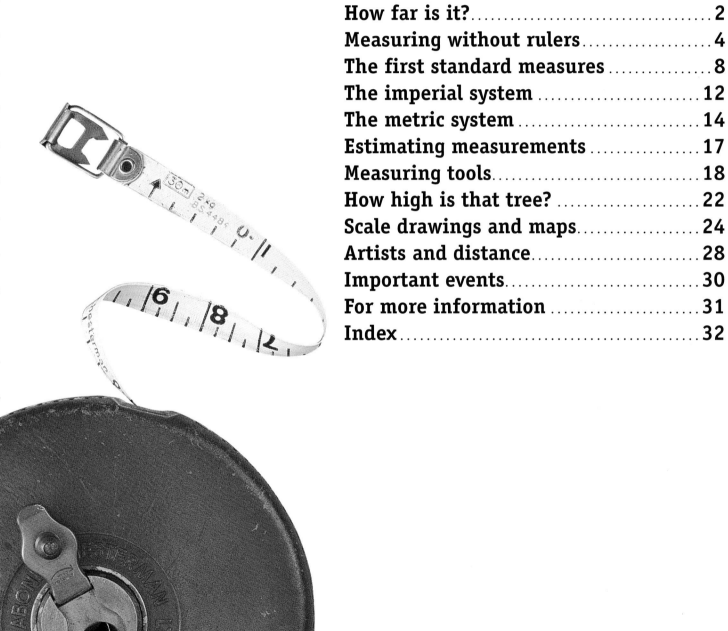

DISTANCE

by Brenda Walpole
Illustrations by Dennis Tinkler
Photographs by Chris Fairclough

Contents

Gareth Stevens Publishing
MILWAUKEE

How far is it?

Every day we use our knowledge of distance. For example, do you know how far it is from one end of this swimming pool to the other, or from one side of the pool to the other?

To answer these questions, you have to figure out the distance between two points. After determining these distances, you can decide how far you want to swim. Length, width, and height are measures of distances.

We can judge distances approximately with our eyes. Objects that are far away appear to be smaller than they really are. A ship on the horizon may look tiny, even though we know it's large enough to carry people. But if you want to find out the winner of a long-jump competition or make sure new shoes fit properly, you have to measure accurately.

Measuring without rulers

Before rulers and tape measures were invented, people used things they always had with them — their fingers, hands, arms, and feet.

Hands are very useful for measuring small distances. You can use the width of your thumb to measure this page. How many of your thumbs does this page measure?

Measuring a tabletop in thumbs would take a long time. It would be better to use spans. A span is the distance between the tip of the little finger and the thumb when the fingers are stretched out. Measure a tabletop in spans. If the table is not an exact number of spans, measure the remainder in half-spans or thumbs.

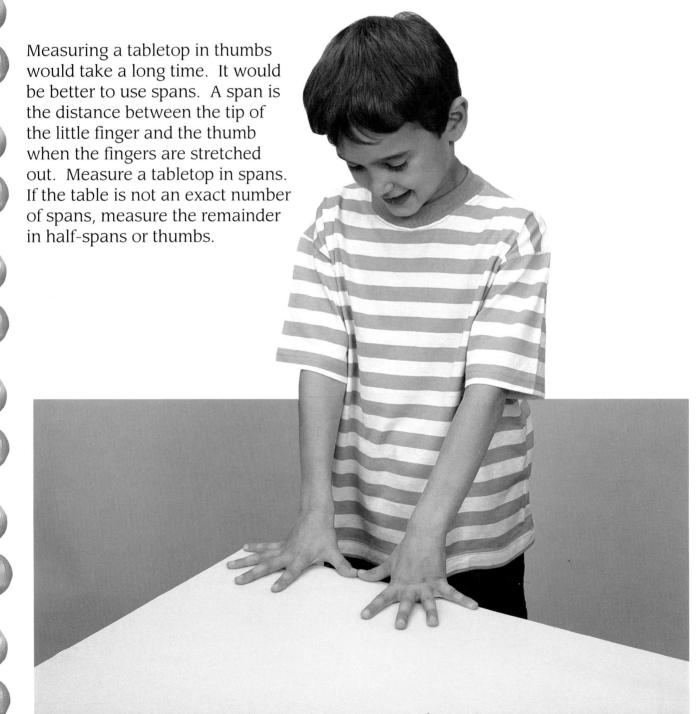

Here are some other body measures you can use to measure distances. Originally, they were based on the body measurements of an average-sized man.

A fathom is the distance between the fingertips, when the arms are stretched out completely.

Half a fathom is the distance between the nose and the middle fingertip of an outstretched arm.

A digit is the width of the middle finger.

A cubit is the distance from the elbow to the middle fingertip.

A palm is the distance from one side of the hand to the other when the fingers are pressed together.

A foot is the distance between the heel and the big toe.

Which body measure do you think would be the best to figure out these distances: the width of a wall map, the height of a tulip, and the width of a playground?

P.S. Make a chalk mark on a wall to show your height. How many of your fathoms fit into your height?

5

Make rulers from your own body measurements with strips of paper, lengths of string, and pieces of wood.

Using your own rulers, figure out:
—how many of your thumbs fit into one span
—how many of your cubits equal one fathom
—how many of your feet equal half a fathom
—how many of your palms equal one cubit
—how many of your feet equal one stride.

Record your findings on a chart and compare your results with your friends. Are they the same?

number of:	Katy	SanJay	Lee
thumbs in a span	11	12	
cubits in a fathom	4		
feet in half a fathom			3
hands in a cubit	4	5	4
feet in one stride		3	

Everyone has his or her own body measures, but most people have body proportions that are about the same. A tall person will have longer legs and bigger feet than a shorter person. But a tall person's stride is the distance of three large feet, and three small feet fit into a smaller person's stride. Usually two spans fit into one cubit.

If you and some of your friends measure the length of a table in spans, you will get lots of different answers because some of you have bigger hands than others. And if you all want to measure lots of different objects and make a chart of your results, your different measurements could make things very confusing.

P.S. Without using an ordinary measuring ruler, how would you solve this problem?

The first standard measures

When people first began measuring distances with their bodies, they soon realized that everyone had different measurements. Many early civilizations developed systems of measurement with a standard size for each measure that everybody used.

In ancient Egypt, one of the most widely used measures was the cubit. In about 3000 B.C., a Royal Cubit was made in black granite. It was the length of the Pharaoh's cubit. Each cubit measuring stick was checked against the Royal Cubit before it was used. The Pyramids of Giza were built by thousands of people, yet all the dimensions of the pyramids were precisely measured because the cubit sticks were very accurate.

The Egyptians also devised one of the first ways of surveying and measuring land. Each year, the Nile River overflowed its banks because of heavy rains. The rains washed away the walls that marked the boundaries to the farmers' fields. When the water drained away, people needed to measure the boundaries again. They used ropes to do this, and the workers were called rope-stretchers. The ropes were knotted at intervals of exactly one cubit.

Be a rope-stretcher

You will need: a long rope knotted into cubit lengths, some friends.

Tie a knot in the rope every cubit length. Make sure the distance between each knot is one cubit exactly.

What is the perimeter of, or distance around, your playground or local park measured in cubits?

The people of ancient China developed a different system of measuring. One standard measure was the distance from the pulse of the wrist to the base of the thumb.

A measuring mess

Thousands of years ago, the ancient Greeks and then the Romans controlled the lands around the Mediterranean Sea. The Greeks used a version of the Egyptian measuring system, with a finger width as the basic unit of length. Sixteen fingers equaled one foot, and twenty-four fingers equaled one cubit.

The Romans made a new system, in which one foot was divided into twelve inches. The Latin word for inch is *uncia*, which means "one-twelfth." Originally, the measurement of the foot was the length of a Roman centurion's sandal.

By medieval times, all the lands around the Mediterranean used the Roman system of feet and inches, but the size of one foot and one inch varied slightly from place to place.

Large trade fairs were held during the twelfth and thirteenth centuries, bringing together merchants from many countries around the Mediterranean. The merchants had to agree to use the same system of measurement so they could buy and sell goods fairly.

Wool merchants from different countries measured their cloth in ells, the distance from the elbow to the fingertip. An iron rod exactly one ell long was kept by the Keeper of the Fair, who checked that the merchants did not cheat.

The imperial system

In England, measuring was confusing because people in different parts of the country and in different trades used different systems. In 1305, King Edward I made a royal order that set standard units of measurement. They were so successful they were used for almost six hundred years. These standard units became known as the imperial, or English, system.

The standard unit of a mile had been used since Roman times. A mile was one thousand paces. The word *mile* comes from the Latin word *mille*, which means "one thousand." A mile was the usual distance between castles along a Roman boundary wall. This nineteenth-century painting shows the remains of a mile-castle on Hadrian's Wall, which divided England from Scotland.

A furlong was set as the distance of one-eighth of a mile. It was as far as a horse could pull a plow without needing a rest. The word *furlong* comes from the Old English word *farlang*, meaning "furrow-long."

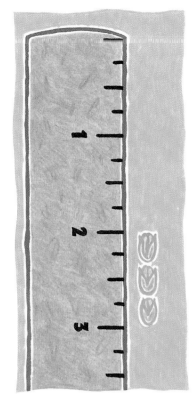

A standard yard, known as the "Iron Yard of our Lord King," was divided into three feet, each twelve inches long. An inch was divided into three barleycorns. This photograph shows a woman in a nineteenth-century draper's shop measuring fabric with a yardstick from that time.

In the seventeenth century, a new unit called a chain was added to the list of imperial measurements. The chain was sixty-six feet long. After this, the imperial system of measuring was complete and was used throughout Britain, the United States, and Commonwealth countries.

Until the beginning of the nineteenth century, each standard measure in England was made into an iron bar and kept in London. Exact copies were made in bronze or brass and sent to other towns. When the copies became worn and inaccurate, new ones were made.

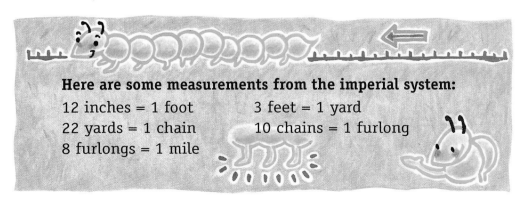

Here are some measurements from the imperial system:

12 inches = 1 foot   3 feet = 1 yard
22 yards = 1 chain   10 chains = 1 furlong
8 furlongs = 1 mile

The metric system

In 1791, a committee of the French Academy of Science defined a new unit of measurement called the meter. The committee measured the distance from the North Pole to the Equator as accurately as possible, and divided this distance into ten million parts. One part was called a meter, or measure. In 1875, the metric system was devised. In France, plaques showing the standard meter were put up in public places, and a standard meter bar of platinum iridium was kept at the town of Sèvres. Since 1960, the meter has been more accurately measured as the length of a certain number of wavelengths of light traveling through pure krypton gas.

Meters are divided into small units so tiny objects can be measured and grouped into big units to measure long distances. Big and small measurements are easier to figure out in the metric system than the imperial system because they are calculated in decimals. All modern scientific instruments use the metric system.

Here are some measurements from the metric system:

1 meter = 100 centimeters

1 centimeter = 10 millimeters

1,000 millimeters = 1 meter

1,000 meters = 1 kilometer

Britain and some Commonwealth countries used the imperial system until 1963, when Parliament decided that the metric system could be used alongside imperial weights and measures.

Over one hundred years ago, the metric system was introduced to the United States, but even today it is used by few people except scientists. The United States uses a closely related version of the imperial system, called the customary, or English, system.

In the United States and some parts of Britain, road signs show distance in miles. Look at these French and British road signs that show distance in kilometers and convert the distances.

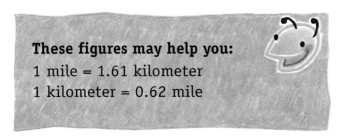

These figures may help you:
1 mile = 1.61 kilometer
1 kilometer = 0.62 mile

P.S. Using a map of the U.S., can you figure out the distance from Chicago to New Orleans in miles and in kilometers?

Choosing the right measure

Which units of measure would you choose to measure a grain of rice, the length of a pencil, and the width of your classroom? First estimate the lengths, and then measure them. Did you estimate correctly?

Very tiny objects, too small for us to see, can be measured in micrometers. A micrometer is one-millionth of a meter. This photograph of bacteria was taken through a powerful microscope that makes the bacteria look much bigger than they really are. Each single bacterium is approximately 1 micrometer in length. The line below shows the length of 1 micrometer at the same magnification.

⊢⊣

Estimating measurements

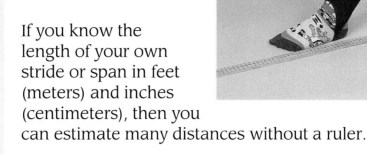

If you know the length of your own stride or span in feet (meters) and inches (centimeters), then you can estimate many distances without a ruler.

Measure your span in inches or centimeters, and then measure a distance in spans. Multiply the number of spans by the number of inches or centimeters in your span.

This woman is 5 feet 7 inches (1 m 70 cm) tall. Estimate the size of the statue she is standing beside.

Ask a friend to stand inside a doorway. Estimate how many times your friend's height fits into the height of the doorway. Measure the height of the doorway. Did you estimate correctly?

Measuring tools

To measure land, surveyors need tools that are flexible, tough, and waterproof. Edmund Gunter, a seventeenth-century English mathematician, made the first surveying chain. It was 66 feet (20.12 m) long and made from one hundred separate links. Every ten links had a different-shaped brass marker that showed its distance from the beginning of the chain. Today, most surveyors use retractable cloth or steel tapes.

Something to try

Make your own measuring chain

You will need: one hundred paper clips, paper, scissors, string.

Link the paper clips together. Cut out ten paper markers, each one a different shape. Every ten links, tie a marker to the chain. Use your chain to measure a variety of objects.

It would take a long time to measure a winding road with a tape measure. It might be easier to use a road measurer.

Something to try

Make a road measurer

You will need: a ruler; a compass; a red felt-tip marker; strong cardboard; about 3 feet (1 m) of narrow, soft wood; scissors; a nut and bolt.

Draw a circle with a radius of 6 inches (15 cm) on the cardboard. Draw the radius of the circle in red. Cut out the circle. With an adult's help, make a hole in one end of the wood and a hole in the center of the circle. Attach the wood to the circle with the nut and bolt.

Your road measurer will have a circumference of about 3 feet (1 m). Roll it along beside you. Every time the red mark reaches the top, you have measured about 3 feet (1 m).

In 1902, Captain Robert Scott and a team of explorers made an expedition to Antarctica. They measured the distance they traveled with a sled geometer, which worked in the same way as your road measurer. The sled geometer was attached to the back of the sled and had spikes that stopped it from sinking into the snow.

19

Calipers measure the inside or outside of unusual shaped objects.

Make your own calipers

You will need: a 12-inch (30.5-cm) ruler, two pieces of strong cardboard for the uprights, modeling clay, paper, a ball, right-angled triangles.

Lay the ruler flat and attach the first upright to the 0 mark with modeling clay. Loop a small band of paper around the ruler, as shown in the picture. Attach the second upright to the paper with modeling clay. Make sure you can slide the second upright along the ruler.

Place the ball against the first upright, and slide the second upright to touch the edge of the ball. What's the diameter of the ball?

P.S. How do you think the triangles will help make your readings more accurate?

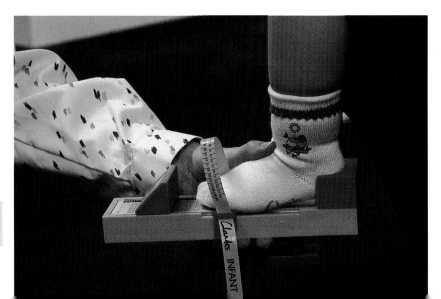

20

Have you seen measuring devices like this at a shoe store?

Instant rulers

When bats fly, they make high-pitched noises that help them judge distances. When the noise hits an object, echoes bounce back. The bat times the delay between making the noise and hearing the echo. A long delay means the object is far away, and a short delay means the object is nearby. This system, called echolocation, is so efficient that bats can fly safely in total darkness.

Satellites that are used to calculate distances work in a similar way. Powerful beams of light are sent up into space where they bounce off the satellites and travel back to Earth.

How high is that tree?

Three different ways to estimate the height of a tree

Measuring-triangle method

Try making a measuring triangle. Use a ruler to draw a right-angled triangle exactly like the one here, with sides that measure 4 inches (10 cm), 4 inches (10 cm), and 5.5 inches (14 cm).

Face the tree and put one point of the triangle to your nose. Close one eye and, keeping the triangle upright, gradually move back until the top point of your triangle seems to be at the top of the tree.

Mark the place where you are standing and measure how far it is from the base of the tree. This distance is the approximate height of the tree. To make your estimate more accurate, add to the distance your own height up to your eye level.

Upside-down method

Stand with your back to the tree and slowly walk away. Bend down and look through your legs. Walk away until you can see the top of the tree. The distance between you and the tree is approximately the height of the tree.

Ancient Egyptian method

Hold the bottom of a pencil and stretch out your arm. Walk back until the pencil just covers the height of the tree. Then turn the pencil to make a right angle. From the base of the tree, the distance on the ground that the pencil appears to cover is the approximate height of the tree. Ask a friend to stand where the point of the pencil appears to fall and measure the distance to the base of the tree.

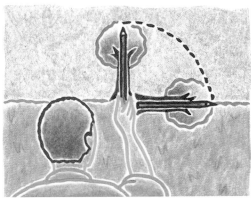

Scale drawings and maps

When we take the measurements of a room or a building, the real distances are too big to draw on paper. To make a drawing of the measurements, all the distances must be reduced by the same proportion. The drawing is accurate, but the picture is much smaller than the real measurements. This is called drawing to scale.

Something to try

Draw this cartoon to a larger scale

Each square in this grid is 2 centimeters x 2 centimeters. Draw a similar grid, but make each square 4 centimeters x 4 centimeters. Then carefully copy, square by square, the cartoon onto your grid. Your cartoon is at a scale of 2:1, which means that 2 centimeters on your drawing represents 1 centimeter on the original drawing.

For your information:
1 centimeter = .394 inches
2 centimeters = .8 inches
4 centimeters = 1.6 inches

Some scale drawings show places and things as they look from above. This is called a bird's-eye view. This photograph of a maze was taken from above. Look at the map of the maze. Can you figure out how to get to the middle? Look for bird's-eye view photographs or maps in shops, museums, and malls.

Designers, mapmakers, and architects call a bird's-eye view a plan view. This is an architect's plan view of a new building, drawn to scale. It shows the size of each room and where the doors and windows are going to be. The architect also makes a scale drawing of the front of the building. This is called an elevation.

P.S. Make a plan view of your bedroom. Use a scale of 1 inch (cm) to represent 1 foot (m).

All sorts of maps and plans are drawn to scale. The size of the scale depends on how much detail and information is needed on the map.

Most maps have the scale marked on them. Look at different maps and see what scales they use. The map of Australia below is drawn to a metric scale of 1:25,000,000. That means 1 centimeter represents 250 kilometers. In U.S. equivalents, 1 inch would equal approximately 395 miles.

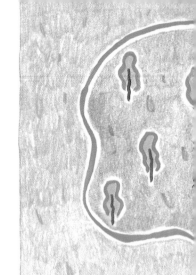

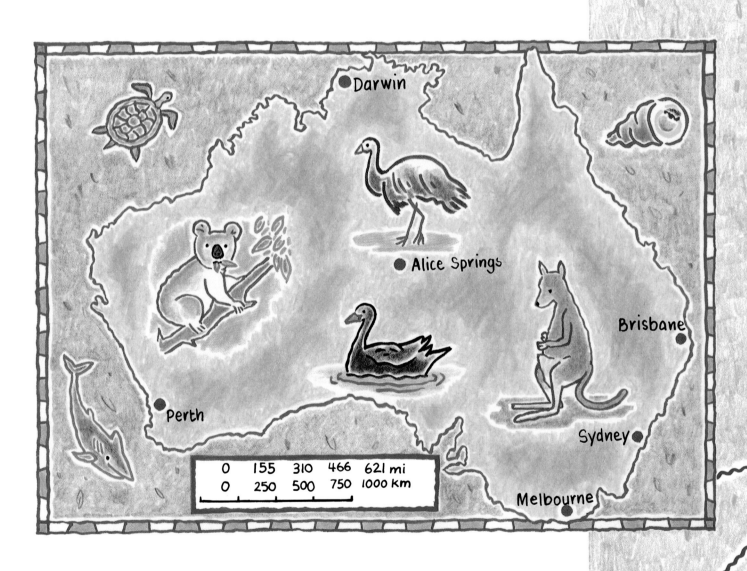

0	155	310	466	621 mi
0	250	500	750	1000 km

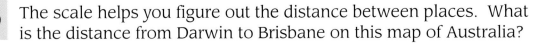

The scale helps you figure out the distance between places. What is the distance from Darwin to Brisbane on this map of Australia?

This road map is drawn to a scale of 1:200,000 and shows more detail than the map of Australia. Some maps use symbols to show features, such as railroad stations, post offices, and hiking trails.

How far is it from Abbeytown to Berryville? If you measure the distance in a straight line, your answer will be 28 kilometers (17.4 miles). But it would be difficult to travel in a straight line because the map shows that the road is long and winding. You could walk from Abbeytown to Berryville on a hiking trail that is a more direct route, although still not straight.

Berry Lake

Berry Wood

Station

Berryville

bridge

bridge

footpath

Abbey

Station

Abbeytown

Abbey Forest

Surveyors use special tools to measure distances when they make maps. This man is looking through a machine that uses light beams to figure out how far away things are.

━━━ road
⌇⌇⌇ river
╌╌╌ hiking trail
┼┼┼┼ railroad
woodland

scale:
0   4   8 Km
|—————————————|
0   2.5   5 mi

Artists and distance

Things that are a long way off appear smaller than they really are, like the ship on page 2. Some artists use this idea when they draw pictures. Objects that are supposed to be far away are drawn much smaller than objects that are supposed to be nearby. This gives an impression of distance and is called perspective. In this painting, the artist has drawn the trees in the distance much smaller than the trees nearby.

Make your own perspective drawing

Start by drawing railroad lines with fence posts at the side disappearing into the distance. To create an illusion of distance, the fence posts at the front of your picture should be tall, and those in the distance should gradually get shorter. You know that fence posts that look shorter are farther away than those that look tall. Your brain uses this information to interpret the picture.

Try to draw another picture using perspective.

Sometimes the brain is misled by what the eyes see. This painting by William Hogarth is called *False Perspective.*

Important events

3000 B.C.
Records show that the Egyptians used the cubit as a standard measure of length. The standard Royal Cubit measured 21 inches (about 53 cm) and was divided into twenty-eight smaller units called digits.

221 B.C.
The first emperor of China, Shih Hung Tio, fixed standard measures of length. The chih measured about 10 inches (25 cm) and the chang about 10 feet (3.05 m).

A.D. 100
Most lands around the Mediterranean used a system of feet, inches, and miles introduced by the Romans.

1305
King Edward I of England set the standards for imperial weights and measures, including the foot and yard.

1528
A German artist, Albrecht Dürer, wrote a book that explained how pictures could be drawn with perspective.

1600
Edmund Gunter, a mathematician and astronomer, divided 66 feet into 100 links and called the new measure a chain. This was considered the first surveyors' measuring chain.

1791
A committee of twelve mathematicians from the French Academy of Science proposed a new decimal system of measuring based on the meter.

1866
The U.S. Congress approved the use of the metric system but did not require its use.

1870
An international conference on the metric system met to update the system. Seventeen nations, including the United States, participated.

1963
In Britain, Parliament decided that the metric system of measuring could be used alongside the imperial system.

1971
A U.S. Congressional study recommended that the United States make a planned conversion to the metric system.

For more information

More things to do

1. Compare your body proportions with these standard body proportions: twelve thumbs equal one span; four cubits equal one fathom; three feet equal half a fathom; four palms or two spans equal one cubit; three feet equal one stride.

2. Find and study a map of your state or country. Use the key to help you determine the distance between various cities you have visited. Does the map include any other information to help you know if your distance calculations are accurate?

3. Visit a local museum and try to find examples of instruments used to measure distance in other parts of the world or from long ago. What materials were used to make these instruments? Are these tools similar to measuring instruments used today?

4. People have always been fascinated by record measurements. The giant sequoia tree can grow to a height of 272 feet (83 m). The longest seaweed is the Pacific giant kelp, which can measure up to 197 feet (60.05 m) long. Mount Everest is the tallest mountain in the world. It is 29,028 feet (8,848 m) high. Find out the names of the longest river and the longest road in the world.

5. In this book, you have read about some of the ways people in the past measured distance. The depth of the sea was measured in fathoms (one fathom is about 2 meters or 6.6 feet). Other measures include a rod, a pole, a perch, and a league. Try to find out what these measures were used for and convert them into metric measurements. Try to find out what is still measured in hands today.

More books to read

How We Learned the Earth Is Round. Patricia Lauber (Thomas Crowell)
Length. Henry Arthur Pluckrose (Franklin Watts)
The Longest and Tallest. Anita Ganeri (Barron's)
Making Metric Measurements. Neil Ardley (Franklin Watts)
Maps and Globes. Jack Knowlton (Thomas Crowell)
Measuring and Maps: Projects with Geography. Keith Lyle (Gloucester)
Time, Distance, and Speed. Marion Smoothey (Marshall Cavendish)

Videotapes

Latitude and Longitude (Encyclopedia Britannica Educational Corporation)
Measuring Is Important (Barr Films)
You Too Can Make A Map (Churchill Films)

Places to visit

Museum of Science and Industry
57th Street and Lake Shore Drive
Chicago, IL 60637

National Museum of Science
  and Technology
1867 Saint Laurent Boulevard
Ottawa, Ontario K1G 5A3

The Smithsonian Institution
1000 Jefferson Drive SW
Washington, D.C. 20560

Franklin Institute
20th St. and the Benjamin Franklin Parkway
Philadelphia, PA 19103

Index

For a free color catalog describing
Gareth Stevens' list of high-quality
books, call 1-800-542-2595 (USA)
or 1-800-461-9120 (Canada).
Gareth Stevens' Fax: (414) 225-0377.

Library of Congress Cataloging-in-
Publication Data available upon
request from publisher.
Fax: (414) 225-0377 for the attention of
the Publishing Records Department.

ISBN 0-8368-1360-X

This edition first published in 1995 by
Gareth Stevens Publishing
1555 North RiverCenter Drive, Suite 201
Milwaukee, Wisconsin 53212 USA

This edition © 1995 by Gareth Stevens,
Inc. Original edition published in 1992
by A & C Black (Publishers) Ltd.,
35 Bedford Row, London WC1R 4JH.
© 1992 A & C Black (Publishers) Ltd.
Additional end matter © 1995
by Gareth Stevens, Inc.

Acknowledgements
Photographs by Chris Fairclough, except
for: pp. 2-3 (t) Paul Ridsdale, CFCL; pp. 8
(t), 9 (t) Michael Holford; pp. 8 (b), 17 (b)
Martyn Cattermole, CFCL; p. 10 Museum
of London; p. 11 Fitzwilliam Museum,
Cambridge; pp. 12 (t), 14, 19 (b) Mary
Evans Picture Library; pp. 12 (b), 13
Beamish Open Air Museum; p. 15 CFCL;
p. 16 Microscopix; pp. 18 (t), 27 Ordnance
Survey; p. 20 (b) Clarks Shoes; p. 21
Bruce Coleman; p. 25 (t) Crown Copyright
and reproduced with permission of the
controller of HMSO; p. 25 (b) Timothy
Hatton Architects; p. 28 Bridgeman Art
Library; p. 29 (t) drawing by Daniel
Walpole; 29 (b) Courtauld Institute of Art;
main cover photo Jack Coulthard, CFCL.

Printed in Mexico
1 2 3 4 5 6 7 8 9 99 98 97 96 95

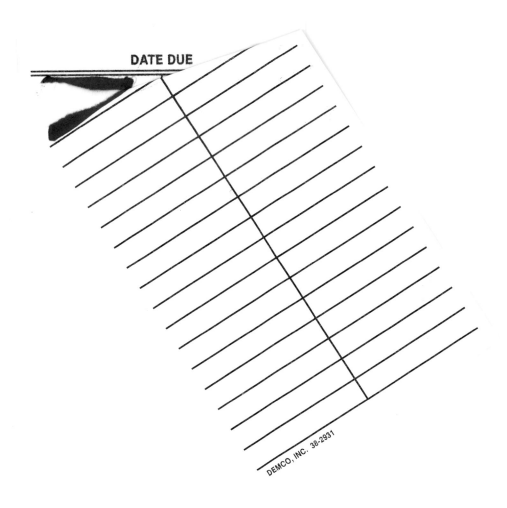

DATE DUE

DEMCO, INC. 38-2931